How to
jump-start
your **sponsorship**
strategy
in tough times

Gail S. Bower

How To Jump-start Your Sponsorship Strategy In Tough Times
Gail S. Bower

The author may be contacted at Gail@GailBower.com.

Printed in USA
ISBN-10: 0-9841006-0-1
ISBN-13: 978-0-9841006-0-6

Credits
Copy editing: Kerry Grombacher
Book and cover design: Brad Wilson

Acknowledgements

I offer my sincere gratitude to all the individuals who informed and inspired this guidebook. To Steven Wood Schmader, International Festival & Event Association, and Penny Reeh, Texas Festival & Event Association, who shared with me the concerns and struggles from the field. To Tim Delaney, National Association of Nonprofits, and Jerry Block, BNY Mellon Wealth Management, for their insights and feedback. To the nonprofit leaders and clients of Bower & Co. Consulting LLC who share with me their most important concerns, challenges, and opportunities. To Dereck Alexander, Traci Browne, Tuesdi Kelly, Mike Staff, and Pam Weisz for sharing their critical sponsorship questions at this time. To George Wein, Quint Davis, and all my colleagues at Festival Productions Inc. of New Orleans, with whom I've learned and shared so much. To my friend and early mentor Anna Zimmerman whose creativity still influences my work today. To Kerry Grombacher and Brad Wilson, the amazing team who helped craft this monograph. And to Barry Vacker, for challenging and encouraging me along the way.

Thank you.

Preface

If you're like many nonprofit and event/festival leaders, you face seemingly overwhelming impediments to securing sponsors. You may be stopped, dead in your tracks, unsure about what – if anything – you can do next. This book is for you.

My goal is to flip your thinking on its side and provide a jump-start, in the form of the tools and techniques – and confidence – you need to go forward.

How to Jump-start Your Sponsorship Strategy in Tough Times paints a picture of the economic events and realities of the last year as they relate to sponsorship. You'll have an understanding of the prevailing trends and challenges that face you *and* your sponsors.

Combined with your knowledge of your organization, event or festival, and what is happening in your own business environment, this guidebook will assist you to:

- navigate the best path to build relationships with current and new sponsors,
- improve the value of your sponsorship opportunities,
- enhance your sponsorship revenue, and
- cultivate the best environment for your sponsorship program to generate results for you and your partners.

I want to support your organization, your event, your conference, or your festival's ability to secure and retain corporate sponsors in the midst of an extremely challenging economic climate.

We have no time to waste. Let's get started!

Gail S. Bower
Philadelphia, Pennsylvania

What Happened?

Despite signs of instability in the markets throughout 2007 and into 2008, economists would finally declare an official recession that, they say, began in December 2007. When the announcement was made in December 2008, a collective "no kidding!" was sounded because most people already had been experiencing the affects of economic turmoil.

No one, however, predicted what would transpire in 2008 and carry over into 2009:

- The collapse of leading investment banking firms (Bear Sterns in March, Lehman Brothers in September 2008);
- The assertion that AIG's potential collapse would cause severe damage to global financial markets and the subsequent four-part multi-billion dollar bailout by the federal government, punctuated by reports of lavish corporate retreats and $165 million in signing and retention bonuses that were owed to executives;
- Bankruptcies, or near bankruptcies, of major national banks (including Washington Mutual, Wachovia);
- A catastrophic freeze of credit, hurting businesses, governments, nonprofits, and individuals;
- The subsequent and shocking appropriation of more than $700 billion in October's Emergency Economic Stabilization Act, otherwise known as the Troubled Asset Relief Program, or TARP. Through TARP, the government is purchasing "troubled assets," such as mortgages and other securities, which may be collateralized, and equity in order to strengthen and stabilize the financial sector (see FinancialStability.gov for details);
- Restrictions imposed by the Treasury on executive compensation for senior executives at companies participating in TARP;

- Massive home foreclosures in some markets, plus a broader plunge in home real estate values;
- Mass layoffs and business bankruptcies, with no discernable pattern related to industry or company size;
- Stock market fluctuations, gyrating 50 percent below the highs, reaching lows not seen in over a decade;
- Bailouts and bankruptcy filings in the stagnating automotive industry (General Motors and Chrysler);
- Signs of economic instability in other parts of the globe, since the world's economic network extends beyond the borders of single countries;
- The shutdowns of multiple major regional newspapers that printed final paper editions and in some cases moved to online distribution: Seattle Post-Intelligencer, Tucson Citizen, Rocky Mountain News in Denver, The Cincinnati Post, South Idaho Press, Ann Arbor New, and others (see newspaperdeathwatch.com for current list);
- Unemployment that, as of this writing, is soaring to more than 13 percent in some states.

The never-ending hemorrhage of bad news, stoked by relentless, sound bite-style media coverage, has created mass uncertainty in the marketplace. Everyone, from teenagers to retirees, has experienced moments of fear and anxiety, even panic, unsure what the future holds and worried that it might be the worst.

The Event that Triggered Legislative Action

In the midst of all of this market upheaval and what the travel industry now calls "The AIG Effect" came another event, this one played out in the political arena and dramatized by the media, that has had the greatest impact on the events and sponsorship industries. In late February 2009, Chicago-based Northern Trust Bank, a recipient of TARP funds, went forward with its sponsorship of a PGA Golf Tournament in Pacific Palisades, CA, the Northern Trust Open. As part of its sponsorship, Northern Trust entertained clients and offered financial seminars for about 2,000 customers from around the world.

Members of Congress reacted swiftly. Eighteen Democratic House Financial Services Committee members co-signed a letter to Northern Trust's President and CEO.[1] A Senator introduced legislation prohibiting companies that receive TARP funds from being allowed "to host, sponsor, pay for conferences and events and pay for holiday or entertainment events for the year in which they receive TARP funds."[2] (When the bill became known officially as "S. 463: TARP Taxpayer Protection and

Corporate Responsibility Act of 2009," the words "conferences" and "events" were deleted from the text.[3])

Calling the sponsorship "another idiotic abuse of taxpayer money," the Senator stated that "some companies clearly need a reality check to get their priorities straight so taxpayer money is used to get their house in order and not to pay for lavish parties."[4]

The Other Side of the Story

As the story unfolded, though, we learned that taxpayer dollars were *not* spent on lavish parties or any other expense related to the golf sponsorship. Fiscally-sound Northern Trust Bank had decided to move forward with the second year of its five-year sponsorship commitment to the PGA, made in 2007 before TARP dollars were even conceived, using "normal operating funds,"[5] unrelated to TARP funds.

Furthermore, we learned that Northern Trust had not requested TARP dollars but agreed to participate in the program, as did many other profitable banks, at the government's request, in an effort to broaden participation in the program. By issuing TARP funding, the government essentially purchased bank shares, which pay dividends.

According to an Open Letter from Frederick H. Waddell, Northern Trust Corporation's President and CEO, which was posted on the financial institution's web site, the government receives "US$78.8 million on an annual basis as a return on taxpayers' investment – almost US$20 million per quarter."[6]

Despite the facts, the damage was done. Politicians and media pundits lobbed sharp but shallow criticism, whipping up a public outcry over this corporate "excess."

> In the midst of all of this market upheaval came another event that has had the greatest impact on the events and sponsorship industries.

9

Bailouts & Politics:
The Effects on the Marketplace and the Sponsorship Sector

Predictably, other companies in the financial industry, including Morgan Stanley, Wells Fargo, and Bank of America, reconsidered their sponsorship commitments.[7] Goldman Sachs and Wells Fargo changed their conference plans, and Citigroup reportedly canceled a contract for a corporate jet.

Though this scrutiny focused on the financial industry, especially those receiving taxpayer funds, there's no doubt that senior leaders in other industries across the country pulled back, reconsidered, and canceled other sponsorship, conference, and client entertainment activities, not wanting to be part of the maelstrom.

Rejecting TARP Dollars

Ironically, the effect is likely to compromise TARP. Goldman Sachs, Northern Trust, US Bancorp, and other sound banks began discussing exiting TARP altogether and repaying the monies issued[8] in the first quarter of 2009 because of the political and taxpayer scrutiny, negative publicity, and the negative impact on their business progress.

In March 2009, Johnson Bank, the third largest bank in Wisconsin, declined $100 million from the U.S. Treasury.[9] According to the *Journal Sentinel* in Milwaukee, the overall costs and the public perceptions about what it means to receive TARP money contributed to the bank's decision. Worried about damaging its brand, the bank's leadership weighed factors such as impact on public relations and the "possible disruption of its culture and role in the community."[10]

Russell C. Weyers, COO of Johnson Financial Group, is quoted as saying, "We're not real interested in having people tell us you can't support the Racine Zoo or the Skylight Opera in Milwaukee or whatever we happen to support."

On June 9, 2009, ten banks, including Northern Trust, received word from the Obama Administration, permitting them to exit TARP.[11]

Negative Impact on Travel & Tourism Industry

The meetings, convention and travel industries have also been negatively affected. Corporations have cut conference and travel plans, causing real economic loss and significant uncertainty for conventions locations, like Arizona, Florida, Hawaii, and Las Vegas. Interestingly, Philadelphia launched a campaign to attract businesses seeking to convene, but in a location not seen as frivolous. With plenty to offer, including some fun counterbalanced with historical educational opportunities, Philadelphia, the convention and tourism campaign touts, offers "Serious Value for Serious Times."

Counterbalancing Voices

Understandably, there have been outcries from leaders in the travel, event, and sponsorship sectors whose constituents will suffer because of this legislative proposal and the surrounding misinformation about conferences. The U.S. Travel Association President and CEO Roger Dow rallied a "grassroots army," supported by Meeting Professionals International, Professional Convention Management Association, National Business Travel Association, International Association of Exhibitions and Events, Site (formerly the Society of Incentive and Travel Executives), Destination Marketing Association International, and American Hotel & Lodging Association. The coalition launched meetingsmeanbusiness.com, armed with facts and figures in an effort to protect the industry and the 2.4 million jobs in the United States that are linked to business travel.

The sponsorship industry has been vocal, though less dramatic and unified. IEG, a leading provider of information on the industry, issued statements and fills its newsletters with key intelligence and insights from the field. The voices of other informed reporters counter the inflammatory and misinformed statements swirling in the media debate.

Fortune magazine's senior editor-at-large Allan Sloan states: "But even by my bash-them-bloody standards, Democrats' attacks on banks that have taken bailout money and continue holding meetings in nice places or sponsoring athletic events are way over the line. Sure, it makes for great sound bites ('You took our money to do what?'). But it's counterproductive, because it will cost taxpayers money and make reviving our financial system more difficult."[12]

The New York Times "Everybody's Business" columnist Ben Stein notes that business meetings "are usually not a waste of time," even if they are held in some sexy location.[13] Rather, he reports, "At the gatherings I attend, men and women fly coach, stay in immense, boxy hotels, start their meeting days at breakfast at 7 a.m. and work through the day until far later than seems reasonable to me. Then they do it again the next day and the day after that, finally enduring the torture of waiting at the airport, next to screaming children, in order to get home."

"These meetings, while burdensome, are helpful to the businesses involved," he continues. "They cannot be entirely replaced with teleconferencing or mass e-mailing. The personal touch, the sharing of facts and secrets face to face, are important."

Could Congress or the Supreme Court conduct their business remotely, using technology, he challenges?

Conflicting language used by the media and the public demonstrates both a lack of understanding about the value and effectiveness of corporate sponsorship and a high degree of cognitive dissonance.

For example, in February 2009, a reporter from London's *The Independent* referred to sponsorship revenue as a "gravy train" (prompting a comment from this author).[14]

Quoting sources who predicted a "sponsorship Armageddon," the article conveys several sources' beliefs that sponsorship is simply about being a good citizen and "brand investment," deals and dollars. The article provides no understanding about why sponsors continue to sponsor.

The general public is even worse. Scour readers' comments sections of online newspaper and magazine articles, and the electronic vitriol flashing back at you is startling. The comments construe what we know as a marketing activity into a luxury, an extravagance for the greedy and reckless.

"[Sic] NO MEANINGFUL ADDITIONAL BUSINESS COMES ABOUT FROM THIS EXCESS," says a commenter going by the user name ritaf, about a blog post on golf sponsorship by TARP-receiving banks on philly.com.[15]

Though Advanta did not receive TARP dollars, Advanta's sponsorship of the spring 2009 Cezanne exhibition at the Philadelphia Museum of Art through its foundation was negatively perceived, according to a *US Banker* article. A small business cardholder, a lawyer whose interest rates had increased this year, called the sponsorship, "'a frivolous venture,'"[16] particularly if it was paid for by proceeds derived by the higher rates. According to statements on its web site, Advanta raised

FIGURE 1

Which sponsorship categories would change consumer confidence levels about corporate America and how

	Increase	Decrease	Same
Sports Event	13%	26%	61%
Arts & Cultural Event	20%	20%	60%
Nonprofit Event or Cause	41%	12%	47%

SOURCE: PERFORMANCE RESEARCH

FIGURE 2

Consumer preferences on sponsorship spending levels by 'stable and profitable' corporations

	Same or More
Sports Event	77%
Arts & Cultural Event	79%
Nonprofit Event or Cause	84%

SOURCE: PERFORMANCE RESEARCH

interest rates for cards held by customers with higher risk profiles as a way of mitigating risk and preserving capital. In June 2009, Advanta took a more drastic step to reduce risk and cancelled new usage by hundreds of thousands of cardholders.

Consumer Perceptions Decline

These are just two examples of comments that reveal the tarnished repute of the corporate sector, following a long year of negative economic news and reporting of business practices. After the publicity surrounding the first AIG bailout (more than $85 billion) and its much ballyhooed (and pre-scheduled) retreat, and the Northern Trust PGA sponsorship – companies and situations that have little in common – consumers' approval of corporate sponsorship activities, especially by companies facing difficulties or in unstable industry sectors, has declined.

According to a late February 2009 study by Performance Research, an independent research company that evaluates corporate sponsorship of sports and special events, one-third of American consumers are paying 'less attention' to corporate sponsorship than they were a year ago.[17] More significantly, 69 percent of respondents have a 'lower approval' rating of American corporations in general than a year ago.

Would a corporation's investment in sponsorship make a difference in improving confidence levels? Not for most people responding to the Performance Research study, though as Figure 1 shows, consumer confidence levels about corporations sponsoring a nonprofit event or cause would improve (41 percent) or stay the same (47 percent). Industry matters: confidence levels would decrease for corporations in the banking (37 percent), investment (36 percent), and domestic automotive (30 percent) industries.

If the company is 'stable and profitable,' survey respondents said their preferences for increased or the same levels of corporate spending for sponsorship should be on sports events (77 percent), arts and cultural events (79 percent), and nonprofit or cause-related events (84 percent). (See fig. 2.)

The good news for nonprofit organizations is that your sponsorship opportunities may present your partners with the image enhancing they need.

What You May Be Experiencing

Closer to home, you may encounter any number of hurdles.
- Delays in decision making for renewals or new opportunities.
- Your sponsorship contact at the corporation may face increased pressure from upper management to:
  - Justify costs, strategic priorities about the program, and the cost/benefit ratios;
  - Sponsor something upper management prefers, despite inappropriate strategic fit;
  - Please more decision makers weighing in on expenditures.
- Sponsors wanting to pull out, pull back, or make changes out of fear of, or pressure from, the marketplace.
- Anti-corporate sentiment that is expressed by or that affects your consumers, board members, constituents, media contacts, community, donors, stakeholders, and even your staff.
- In the face of news that corporate sponsorship and corporate giving have dropped precipitously, you may assume that there's nothing you can do about it.

You may experience the same trends and perceptions at the local and regional levels that others face nationally and internationally. The details and extent of the impact may vary depending on your sector, the nature of your sponsorship opportunity, and what's going on in your market.

For example, geographic markets with greater volatility or greater loss, because they are dependent on sole industries, may show greater variance in rates of new and renewing sponsorships than those that are more stable. Or, if your event or festival relies on sponsorship revenue from sources that are experiencing the most turmoil during this period, quite naturally that upset will extend to all business functions, including marketing.

A vortex of economic, political, and market factors, these are the conditions that hang like a slow-moving and low-hanging cloud over a city skyline. The fog will lift, but we don't know when.

Here's the Deal

These are unprecedented times. Sure we've had other recessions before, but during most of our professional lifetimes, we've not witnessed anything like this one. Besides anxiety and uncertainty about our futures, we're experiencing a loss of trust, particularly in those institutions we believed were safest and that safeguarded us, our families, and our communities. People are angry and frightened, facing job losses and diminished equity in their homes and retirement accounts. We're less confident about fulfilling our dreams for the future—from vacation plans to retirement plans.

But at this moment, it's important to restore our own confidence. The world has not come to an end, the economy has not utterly collapsed, and corporate sponsorship has not gone away. The United States is still the leading economy in the world, and about 90 percent of Americans are employed. As of this writing, consumer confidence is already on the upswing; the May report shows an increase of 54.9 percent, the highest level since September 2008.[18]

Have we hit the bottom? Who knows? Will life be different when stability returns? Probably, but life is ever-changing. We can only adapt and set our own directions.

Much of these circumstances is out of your control. You cannot, for example, turn the economy around by yourself, nor can you force your corporate community to invest in your sponsorship program. However, there is much you can do, and what follow are ideas and suggestions about setting a more positive and fruitful path for your corporate sponsorship program.

Six Important Considerations

Before we move on to what is in your control and the steps you can take right now, please keep these important considerations in mind. These points will allow you to counter the power and persuasiveness of the current political and media discourse. They will bolster your skills in persuasion and provide you with the confidence to move forward, for the sake of your event and organization *and* for your partners' sakes.

1. What do we mean by the term "corporate sponsorship"?

When you read references to "corporate sponsorship" in this guidebook, the term is referring to "marketing-driven corporate sponsorship," not work with corporate foundations or the securing of corporate gifts, though a charitable contribution may be tied into the sponsorship investment or related activities. Corporate sponsorship is the investment a corporation makes in exchange for real value that helps them meet business or marketing goals.

IEG defines corporate sponsorship as "a cash and/or in-kind fee paid to a property (typically in sports, arts, entertainment or causes) in return for access to the exploitable commercial potential associated with that property."[19] Corporate sponsorship is distinct from both philanthropy and advertising, though it may offer the goodwill that is associated with philanthropy, and it may include quantifiable components and benefits. Certainly sponsorship decisions must be based on sound rationale, using both qualitative and quantitative measures.

2. Sponsorship is a marketing activity.

Just as advertising, publishing a web site, issuing a press release, or distributing posters are all marketing activities, designed to build awareness and stimulate

19

some action, corporate sponsorship is a tactic or tool from the marketing arsenal. Corporations use sponsorship to deliver messages in particular ways, just like they buy radio spots or lease billboards.

Corporate sponsorship has the power to provide the experience of a product or service in environments that are most conducive, and in ways that are emotionally resonant, for the consumer.[20] Because of this power, sponsorship can be an extremely effective tool to achieve the following outcomes:

1. Increasing sales of a product or service, either before, during, or after the sponsored event.
2. Increasing exposure of a product, service, or brand.
3. Persuasion and developing influence with the public, investors, and other stakeholders or important audiences.
4. Entertaining clients, helping business leaders build new or existing customer relationships and develop client loyalty.
5. Building awareness of the product, service, brand, or issues and values important to a brand.
6. Launching a new product or service.
7. Developing goodwill by visibly making positive contributions to the community.
8. Subtle endorsement by a leader or leading organization in an area.
9. Generating leads.
10. Gathering market data about a target audience.
11. Opportunities for activities and benefits that are very particular, at a granular level, to a business.
12. Volunteerism opportunities.
13. Attracting and retaining customers and clients.
14. Building traffic, either to a bricks-and-mortar location or to a web site.
15. Establishing "thought leadership" so that a person or business is perceived as an expert or authority or at the leading edge of an industry.
16. Recruiting or attracting and retaining top talent. (Even though it seems that businesses of all sizes are letting employees go in droves, as of April 2009, there were 2.5 million jobs available in the marketplace, according to the U.S. Bureau of Labor Statistics' most current report.)
17. Providing access to the your audiences in meaningful ways.
18. Supporting corporate social responsibility initiatives.

Aren't these the outcomes that all businesses want to achieve right now, especially during a tough economy?

3. Corporations are your partners.

Businesses are run by people who live in, enjoy, and avail themselves of all a community has to offer. Corporate leaders support arts and cultural events and organizations, for example, because the arts and culture add to the quality of life of a town, city, and region. Their employees are more interesting and interested individuals because of their exposure to artistic works.

In a recent article in *Time* magazine, author Bob Diddlebock noted that support may be challenging during this economy, "But executives believe the arts are a good investment, a relatively inexpensive brand polisher, as well as a community-development engine and a key to promoting a region as a good place to live and do business.."[21]

The same argument may well be made for the events, functions, and activities of hospitals, social service agencies, disease and healthcare organizations, education organizations, and animal agencies, to name but a few. Nonprofits contribute to the well being of our communities.

Ditto for major annual festivals and cultural and heritage celebrations that bring neighborhoods together.

Now what if your organization or event doesn't have a place – say it's a national or global conference or you bring people together online, no matter where they live? You still have a community, and your organization brings those people together for a purpose. Some faction of the corporate sector is interested in being part of that group and has a vested interest in seeing to the quality of its life.

4. Recognize the value of your sponsorship opportunities.

You need to be able to describe the value your organization offers that will help businesses reach their goals and priorities. Your sponsorship program must customize opportunities to your sponsors' needs, which may have shifted in response to the new realities of our economy. And they may shift again as businesses prepare for the rebound.

Given what just happened and current consumer perceptions:

- ***Don't you think banks need customers?***
- ***Don't you think businesses want to increase sales?***
- ***Don't you think investment firms need to restore the trust of new and existing wealth management clients?***
- ***Don't you think the corporate sector has an image problem that needs to be improved?***
- ***Don't you think the companies need the top talent in their fields to correct problems, innovate, and recalibrate, to propel their businesses forward?***

Of course!

Don't you think your event, festival, program, conference, cause marketing campaign, or activity could help them tackle these objectives?

5. It's not only about your revenue.

One of the biggest mistakes made by sponsorship sellers, particularly those in the nonprofit sector, is to focus on what's in it for them. Face it, Sponsorship Sellers. You want the money.

One of my clients calls this "commission breath." This is a condition in which the salesperson is so eager to make the sale, to get the money, or their commission, that they emit energy that focuses only on making the sale. Maybe you've experienced this yourself. Sponsors – just like anyone being sold something – feel the heat of that commission breath, they know when they're being sold, and they turn off.

Now is not the time for focusing exclusively on your gain. Actually, that's never an effective selling strategy. Your focus must be on what your sponsor needs, and what your two organizations can do together that will meet the corporation's business goals and, of course, your own strategic priorities.

Your sponsors are your "corporate clients," and your sponsorship program is the set of "services" you provide them as a way of connecting with and furthering your mission.

6. Be realistic.

This economy is not an easy time to be in sponsorship sales. It's not impossible, but it is challenging. Recessionary times usually cause businesses to pull back on marketing (and other) spending, including for sponsorship.

In its March 9, 2009, newsletter, IEG reported that 14 percent of corporations are increasing their sponsorship spending; 36 percent will keep it the same; and 51 percent plan to decrease spending.[22] The report also notes that 60 percent intend to consider new sponsorship opportunities this year, a sign, says IEG, that corporations may be looking for less expensive options.

Important evidence for you to have in your back pocket supports the more counterintuitive notion that recessionary times are exactly when marketing spending should hold steady or increase. Research dating from the Great Depression[23] shows that businesses that did just that "saw their sales hold up significantly better than those which didn't," according to a recent article by James Surowiecki in *The New Yorker*.

Sponsorship in the United States and Canada is estimated for 2009 to be a $16.79 billion industry, a 1.1 percent increase over 2008, according to data released by IEG in June 2009.[24] Globally, the report says, the growth rate will be 3.1 percent. Both figures are less than IEG's original projection for 2009; however, they still represent an increase over last year.

Remember that there is money out there, and you have to make the case that the value you have to offer is worth a company's investment. You also have to be realistic and take a long-term perspective. If your sponsors value your sponsorship opportunities, you owe it to them and your property to figure out, together, how to get through this difficult time.

How you manage your relationships with your current partners and set about finding new ones will make a difference in the long run. Panic and complacency are not effective responses. Taking a bold, proactive leadership approach is. Indeed, it's incumbent upon you.

20 Strategies for Sponsorship Success Now

How you go forward will say a lot about you and your organization and about how fit you are to be a partner with the corporate sector. Remember, the key word is partner. Now is the time to step to the plate, demonstrate your leadership skills, and be a good and worthy partner.

At the core of your success in sponsorship development is your ability to take a consultative approach. The only way to do that is to first establish a trusting relationship. Nothing builds trust more than having your partner's best interests at heart.

Here then are the steps you can take right now to jump-start your success with your current sponsors, find new sponsors, and to improve both your sponsorship program and your operation.

5 Ways to Work with Current Sponsors

With your current sponsors, you have an opportunity to deepen your relationships with your contacts, strengthen the ties and all the ways your two organizations are interconnected, and enrich the sponsorship program for your partners and for your own organization. Now is the time for a deeper commitment to your sponsors.

1. Look At the Landscape

If you haven't been doing this all along, take some time to develop an understanding of what your sponsors face in their respective industries and markets.

- Visit your sponsors' web sites.
- Do a web search on each sponsor and each industry segment.
- Regularly read local business publications, the business sections of your local newspaper, and national newspapers, such as *The Wall Street Journal, Los Angeles Times,* and *The New York Times.*
- Read the comments sections of articles you find online.
- Set up Google Alerts and/or a Google News page with your sponsors' names or industries so you stay apprised of news in real (media) time.
- Do a search in Twitter and other social media networks, to find out what your sponsors' customers may be saying.
- Actively use your IEG Sponsorship Report (SR) subscription to conduct searches in the online archives that will help you find current news and trends that involve your clients, their competitors, and their industries.
- Pay attention to advertising.
- Keep your "marketing radar" alert when you are out in the world shopping, traveling, going to other events, and just normally living your life.

These methods are all excellent ways for you to collect information that you will be able to use in your discussions with sponsors.

Here's what you're looking for:

- **Problems in the sector:** bankruptcies, mergers, earnings reports, scandals, polling data that indicates negative perceptions, poor online reputation management, new regulations or changes in governmental affairs.
- **Opportunities in the sector:** mergers, acquisitions, earnings reports, polling data that includes positive and negative perceptions, new product launches, new services, expansions into new markets, new marketing campaigns or promotions, important initiatives, and key messages to stakeholders, investors, shareholders, and other audiences.
- **Ideas:** Take note of what your sponsors' competitors and businesses in other geographic markets may be doing at this time. What appears to work or not work about these ideas? Take note, too, of what organizations like yours in other locales are doing to address sponsorship issues.

Keep files of this information and pay attention to particular trends or notions that resonate for you. What seems important? What seems like an opportunity? What seems troublesome?

2. Talk to Your Sponsors

With this newfound information, contact your sponsors and schedule time with them, preferably in person. Your primary goal is to listen. Find out what's *really* going on with your client's company and with your contact.

Organizational Connections

Your conversation with your sponsor contact is a very important one on both strategic and tactical levels. But there is another conversation that is also important.

Your organization's senior leadership should strive to cement relationships with your sponsors' upper management. That is, the president, executive director, or executive producer of your organization or festival should meet with your sponsors' senior management. If you are the executive director, invite the support of your board chair and/or key members of your board. The conversations are similar in nature to your conversation with

Good Questions to Ask Current Sponsors

1. How is business?
2. What is going on inside the company?
3. What's changed in the last year?
4. What effects has the recession had on your business?
5. What effects has the recession had on your customers' lives?
6. How have these effects altered the way you market your products or services?
7. What pressures are you facing, both externally and internally?
8. How has your organization modified its business strategies?
9. How have these new strategies had an impact on your marketing goals?
10. What promotional opportunities are you focusing on now?
11. Are there crises or public relations challenges you're facing?
12. What pressures do you face from upper management?
13. What are the pressures on upper management?
14. What pressures do you and upper management face from outside audiences?
   a. Governmental?   d. Customers?
   b. Environmental?   e. Community?
   c. Vendors?
15. What worries you? What keeps you up at night?
16. What restrictions or guidelines have emerged that have affected your marketing and sponsorship efforts?
17. In my research of your industry, I learned _____.
   a. I'm wondering how that affects you.
   b. I'm wondering if you see that as an opportunity.
   c. I'm wondering if you see that as a problem.
18. What changes are you making in your sponsorship program?
19. Are you applying different metrics to sponsorship effectiveness?
20. Are there changes in your budgeting and sponsorship selection process for the coming year?

BONUS: How can we collaborate to improve our sponsorship program to better meet your goals and objectives for the coming year?

your key sponsor contact, and the goals are to demonstrate regard for your partners' best interests, to better understand the business climate, and to uncover opportunities for your sponsorship program to make a difference and effect some change or improvement for your corporate clients.

Your goal here is to strengthen the already existing trusting, collaborative, and mutually beneficial relationship with each of your sponsors – organization-to-organization and person-to-person. Your efforts should demonstrate that you value their investment in your event or program, and that you're a worthy partner who is willing and able to be flexible and nimble for the benefit of the long-term sponsorship relationships.

3. Work With Sponsors To Craft The Sponsorship Opportunity

Based on all that you've learned from the sponsor conversations and through your research, how can your program address, alleviate, ameliorate, mitigate, and/or take advantage of these circumstances?

In your discussions with your sponsors – either during this first meeting or after you've returned to your office and discussed your ideas with your colleagues, staff or management – determine what alterations, additional value, reorganization of value or benefits, and new programs would be appropriate. Work with your sponsors to develop these ideas, flesh them out, and determine the implications. Strive to create ideas and activation opportunities that address as many of the client's circumstances as possible, integrating as many goals as possible.

For example, automotive companies have been promoting buy-back guarantees. If a new car buyer loses his or her job after purchasing a new vehicle, the manufacturer will buy it back. If your festival's automotive sponsor has such a guarantee or offer, what can you do within your current operation to promote that offer?

Can you include a short video with the auto company's president speaking directly to your audiences? Can you promote hourly five-minute sessions at the auto company's display area at your festival where the public can learn more about the guarantee? Can you motivate your audiences to take a test drive, with the incentive of a free ticket to your festival and the manufacturer's buy-back guarantee? Can you loop in the HR specialists of your two companies or a noted HR expert in your region to sweeten the threat-of-job-loss-deal even more: the ticket, the buy-back guarantee, and a free coaching session to polish the customer's resume and interviewing skills?

In another example, let's say your nonprofit has a bank sponsor. Even fiscally sound banks risk being perceived negatively these days because of the trust issues and the spillover effects from the problems encountered by other banks, insurers, investment firms, and financial institutions. The public may perceive that all banks are on the verge of collapse, which is not remotely the case.

What can your organization do to restore confidence among your audiences and to demonstrate the health of your fiscally sound bank sponsor? Can you provide your bank sponsor with the opportunity to educate your constituents about some facet of the economy, to improve their own financial literacy or their financial positions? Can you help your bank sponsor engender a greater sense of trust in your community?

In a final hypothetical example, let's imagine that your organization has strong ties to political leaders or government officials on the city, state, or federal level. And let's suppose that your sponsor has an active government relations initiative that now addresses issues caused by the current economic and political turmoil. How can you build bridges? How can you showcase your sponsor in a positive light, in a relaxed setting, to allow the political leaders to hear the sponsor's story.

These ideas are not suggesting that your organization take over your sponsors' marketing functions. Rather, they are meant to inspire meaningful ideas that will address your sponsors' real issues and priorities. The ideas, of course, must work within your operational parameters as well.

4. Measure the Return

Everybody right now is questioning the value of each expense. Personal, corporate, institutional, and governmental budgets are being reviewed with fine-toothed combs. Expenses that remain in the budget are those that have a return and that offer significant value.

Measuring the value of corporate sponsorship can be tricky because it is often not quantifiable. Because its value is largely intangible and qualitative, direct measurement, especially for a one-year deal, can make corporate representatives who are data-driven and analytically oriented wary. Worse, it causes some senior leaders to dismiss the validity of sponsorship outright.

Make sure that you understand how your sponsor plans to measure the return or value of its sponsorship program. Talk with the corporation's senior management about what is realistic, address those needs appropriately with your sponsor contact, and take joint accountability

DO

- Solve a problem.
- Work with the company's PR staff to ensure that there are no additional exposure issues.
- Encourage your sponsor to be candid, so you understand all the issues and aren't blindsided.

DON'T

- Create a bigger problem, exposing the sponsor to more risk.
- Forget to be transparent in your efforts. Customers aren't stupid, and social media remind us each day. Reporters, too, see right through thinly veiled PR tricks.
- Push the idea. If it doesn't come together naturally, organically, don't force it.

for making sure you meet those goals. You don't want to be surprised next year.

If your sponsor's goals are to build awareness for a new product or service and to collect leads, then you must develop and the sponsor must adequately execute a means to collect the appropriate data. If you simply allow them to place logo-identified banners around the festival grounds and mention them in promotional materials, they will not accomplish their goals. These tactics will not achieve the desired results. At the end of the festival, your sponsor will have no leads. This may be an extreme or absurd example, but without clear objectives from the sponsor, your organization cannot incorporate the appropriate components into the sponsorship program.

Coming up with the ideas and offering the rights are just the beginning. If you know that lead-development is important and you put the appropriate program in place, check in with your client periodically throughout the event or the execution of the program (for example, if it's executed online) to make sure it's working. Add stage announcements if you must. Recruit volunteers to encourage festivalgoers to visit your sponsor's booth. Offer to send an email blast after the festival is over or during the online promotion, suggesting that your customers visit your sponsor's web site or retail location.

You and your sponsor must monitor and analyze the program during the event. You will jeopardize your rela-

tionship with the sponsor and the revenue from that partnership if you don't know until your sponsorship program is up for renewal that the sponsor was unhappy or did not derive value. Do what it takes to get the results they need, within reason. Obviously, if your client has poorly planned or executed its own activation activities, ignoring your recommendations, that is out of your control but worrisome nonetheless. Politely note these recommendations in a post-event evaluation and address them for the following year.

5. Renewal Deals.

If you've negotiated your current sponsorship agreement based on meeting business objectives, you have less to worry about than if you did not. Nonprofit organizations that only offer enhanced charitable contributions as sponsorship opportunities, such as the ubiquitous Gold, Silver, and Bronze Packages that are generic and not based on a corporate partner's goals, would seem to have more at risk. (See page 38 for techniques to improve the value of your sponsorship offerings.)

If your program is based on your sponsors' unique objectives, consider these important factors, which may influence your sponsors' decisions to renew.

Check in. During your event, or throughout the duration of your partner's sponsorship program, check in periodically to make sure everything is running smoothly, the sponsor has everything needed, and your contact and management are pleased, if not delighted, with the results.

Evaluation. Be sure to conduct an evaluation after your event or sponsorship opportunity draws to a close so you get a sense immediately for how well your program measured up. Discuss what could be improved or expanded for next year and brainstorm ideas on how that would happen. Be sure to include ideas that engage and benefit the corporation at multiple levels: retail, marketing, PR, sales, HR, and senior management.

Early renewal. Discuss renewal early with your sponsor contact along with new factors (see list of good questions on page 25) that will affect the next year's program. Together, decide how to alter, expand, or even streamline the sponsorship program to best meet the next year's goals. Offer a discount for renewing early.

Manage the process. Determine together when you will submit the proposal or agreement for next year's sponsorship and when you will follow up to answer questions, confirm renewal, and determine next steps. Be sure you know who will make the decision, in case something has changed, and when any internal budget planning occurs so your program is included in the plans. If a new decision maker is involved, be sure to meet with him or her and learn this individual's priorities.

Good proposal. Make sure your proposal outlines the objectives, metrics, and the ROI to your sponsor so that the value is clear.

If your sponsor mentions a reduction in budget or questions fees, here are ways to address that issue:

Budget or cash flow? First, find out if the budget challenge is funding or cash flow. For example if your event or sponsorship opportunity is at the start of a fiscal year, but payment of the fees would happen in the previous year, suggest flexibility on payment terms. Accept more of the payment in the new fiscal year (but before your event).

Protect value. Do not reduce fees without reducing commensurate value. Period. You must maintain the value of your sponsorship program for the best interests of all your sponsors. If the corporation does need to reduce its investment in your program, is there a way that you can streamline the program, eliminating tertiary and even secondary benefits that are not directly related to the sponsor's primary objectives? Or is there another opportunity, perhaps a lower level option, that may still meet the sponsor's objectives? Examples might include going from a main stage sponsorship to a smaller stage sponsorship; from title or presenting sponsor to a main stage or conference track sponsor; or from an official product to a stage sponsor level.

Ramifications. Discuss the ramifications of this change in commitment level with your partner. What will it mean to the sponsor's visibility at the event? What are the PR ramifications and how might you help mitigate any downside to the decision to scale back the sponsorship?

In-kind value. Finally, don't be afraid to explore ways your sponsor may pay its fees, even partially, in other forms. Don't go into a long sob story about how financially destitute your event or organization will be if the sponsor cuts back. Remember it's not all about *you*; your sponsors are your clients, your corporate customers. Furthermore, that kind of discussion sends red flags about your organization's financial stability and alerts your sponsor to the potential risk of investing in your event.

Instead, agree to accept other forms of payment. Is there an in-kind contribution of product or service the sponsor may make, something that will be useful and offset hard costs in your budget? Could the sponsor pick up other costs for the event, such as printing or postage, web site design, or advertising costs? Or provide the venue for a meeting or small conference?

Be creative, but make sure you're not accepting as a fee something that has no value to you. For example, samples of a client's product that you may use as a give-away have great value to the sponsor – you're putting their product into potential customers' hands – but no value to you. You can't pay the musicians or the security costs with thousands of samples of a consumer product.

In-kind products or services can be a terrific benefit to you. There are only two ways to turn a profit: lower expenses or increase revenue. Your sponsors can help you with both. However, to take full advantage of these opportunities, which may be necessary during this economy to preserve these relationships, you have to work months in advance to allow for proper coordination. You cannot begin contacting sponsors, new or renewing, two months before the event – nor should you in even the best of times – because you will not allow enough time to coordinate these exchanges.

5 steps I'll take with my current sponsors:

1. _____
_____
_____

2. _____
_____
_____

3. _____
_____
_____

4. _____
_____
_____

5. _____
_____
_____

5 Suggestions for Securing New Sponsors

1. What Opportunities Do You See?

Bring a discerning eye, along with a healthy dose of creativity, to your exploration for new sponsor possibilities. As you monitor the media, interact with the business world, and go about your daily life, look for signs of new life and evidence that maybe there's another way of looking at things.

Not every industry sector, nor every business in troubled sectors, has collapsed. Some are doing quite well. However, with the constant onslaught of negative news, it's easy to assume otherwise. Your job is to look for the opportunities, the signs of new life emerging from the rubble. By flipping a situation around, you may begin to see opportunities where others don't.

For example, a company that has image issues, or is intent on building its customer base, though left for dead by the media, may very well make a good sponsor for you. Can you assist the business with these image issues? Are your customers potentially their customers? Can you motivate your customers to visit their stores and web site?

You probably don't want to approach a company that is clearly having serious problems, like AIG or General Motors, for example. But what other insurance companies or automobile manufacturers have potential? And within those industries what do you see?

Take the automotive sector, for example. Gasoline prices and concern about the impact of our use of fossil fuels on the environment are changing America's car buying and usage patterns. *The New York Times* reported that new car sales are expected to decline; however, participation in urban car sharing programs is on the rise.[25]

Is car sharing a new category that urban nonprofit organizations and festivals might approach? What about manufacturers or distributors of scooters or public transit authorities? If people are keeping cars longer, does that mean that auto parts, or major maintenance and repair businesses, are a category worth exploring?

Take a probing look at what you're seeing. Then research your hunch. Do a web search on the industry to see if trade publications have anything to say about new trends. Visit IEG's web site, sponsorship.com, to see what they've uncovered. If your hunch is corroborated, make inquiries in these sub-sectors, building your business case around your sponsorship opportunity.

You may need to spend extra time educating business people in sub-sectors that have not previously been active in the sponsorship arena. It's in your interest to talk with them about the value of sponsorship, compared to other marketing methods, and to be particularly realistic about their expectations for returns. The extra effort may be worth the rewards of cultivating new partners.

2. OTHER IDEAS.
Who's In The News? Who's Advertising?

Search the news for other opportunities. For example, check your local newspapers. Banks are advertising free checking, good rates, and all sorts of incentives to open new accounts. Obviously, they're looking for new customers.

Homeowners have been refinancing their mortgages. Consumers are looking for thrifty shopping and dining alternatives. Wal-mart and Target, McDonalds and KFC all seem to be meeting their needs. Rather than buying new homes, many Americans are electing to stay put; they may need the services and products of home improvement businesses. People splurge on pets, no matter the economy. And, people still need the basics – consumer packaged goods, gasoline, and healthcare, to name a few.

Good Questions to Ask New Sponsors

1. What is the decision making process at your company?
2. Whose budget or budgets does sponsorship impact?
3. Who will be involved in making this decision?
4. What are your sponsorship goals?
5. What are you trying to accomplish through sponsorship with us?
6. How do you measure the success of a sponsorship?
7. What are the best methods for securing business in your industry?
8. When are the peak sales periods in your business?
9. How long is the selling cycle in your business?
10. What are some effective techniques to close that selling cycle?
11. What effect has the recession had on your business?
12. What effect has the recession had on your customers' lives?
13. How have these impacts altered the way you market your products/services?
14. What marketing challenges do you face?
15. What marketing opportunities are ahead: product launch, redesign, push?
16. What is your most difficult business challenge for the year ahead?
17. Who are the decision makers you try to reach?
18. What are the most important corporate sponsorship benefits to you?
19. What types of events do you usually sponsor? Why do you choose them?
20. Will you use this sponsorship opportunity to build awareness, or is there a measurable return that you seek?

You get the idea. Look at who's advertising right now and how; what are the messages they're trying to convey? How could these message work, or be delivered more effectively, through sponsorship?

Grocery Store Discoveries

As you're pushing your cart through the grocery store, look for new product introductions and new brands. Recessions can actually be a good time to launch new products and businesses. Which of these might benefit from an association with your sponsorship program?

3. MORE IDEAS.

Obama's Hopes

President Obama campaigned with pledges of commitment to three initiatives: affordable healthcare for everyone; reducing dependency on foreign oil supplies and increasing alternative energy sources; and boosting employment through funding shovel-ready infrastructure improvement projects.

Do you see any opportunities there? Do you have an opportunity that might be just right for one of these categories? Is there a new program or activity you may be able to innovate? Do you have ideas on your wishlist that might be ready for development, with participation from one of these sectors?

Small and Medium-Sized Businesses

Don't just look at the Fortune 500. Small and medium-sized businesses also market their brands and have just as much to gain from sponsorship as the big guys.[26] Sure, they're not coming in with multi-million dollar sponsorship packages, but you may be able to cultivate certain businesses by creating entry-level packages in the four- and five-figure range.

Educating the business owner or senior leadership about expectations and delivering clear value and tangible returns will be key.

4. Approach with New Sponsors

Potential sponsors to your event, festival, conference, or nonprofit program may be skittish about making new investments. Be realistic. If your sponsor opportunity or event is new, you have even more to prove.

- **Reduce risk.** You're an unknown entity to this new sponsor; why should it invest with you? Your conversation, materials, and your event itself must address this question and overcome the perceived risks. Here are just a handful of the questions that will likely be going through your contact's mind:

- Can I really trust this person and the organization?
- Will he/she deliver good customer service?
- Will he/she really help us achieve our desired outcome?
- Will he/she help us develop realistic expectations?
- Is your event successful? Who says?
- Will you invest adequately in advertising and marketing so the attendance is really what you say it will be?
- Do other sponsors really get the results you say they do?
- How much will it cost?
- Is it worth the money?
- **Focus on the long term.** If your focus is simply transactional, you'll have "commission breath." Instead, focus on introducing this business to your organization, to your event, to you, and perhaps even to sponsorship itself. Focus on building trust and rapport. Set your goals for a long-term relationship.

Certainly, there may be an opportunity to cultivate this new sponsor for the upcoming event. But if the timing is off, or the business is unable or unwilling to redirect resources to your event, invite the contact and colleagues or guests to be *your* guest at your next event. Stay in touch until then, and when they arrive at your event, take them on a tour, point out interesting activation ideas, introduce them to other key (and satisfied) sponsors. Help them to imagine the potential that exists for their brand.

5. Network

Boost your networking activities right now to meet new people with the decision-making authority to invest in your sponsorship program. Here are ten sources to expand your network:

1. Ask your current sponsors. Who else can they refer to you?
2. Check with your media partners, especially through their advertising sales staff. These folks know who's advertising. How can you make it worthwhile to them to ask for an introduction? For example, could you offer an incentive or an expanded media buy if their client signs on?
3. Check with retail partners, who know about new products, which manufacturers have co-op budgets to spend, and which are more promotionally minded than others. Who can they help you bring to the table? Retail partners benefit from increased traffic and sales resulting from the sponsorship effort.
4. Reach out to your board and circle of influence. Who do your board members know? Who among your staff

jump-start

members' connections might be appropriate sponsors? Follow these network links until you get to the right person.

5. Do you know who the right person is, but don't know how to reach them? Enter the name in LinkedIn and see who in your network knows them. Make the connection, but not electronically. Pick up the phone. Human contact is always best. Use other social networks to conduct research in similar ways.

6. Attend and support business and fundraising events in your community. You'll meet a new world of business contacts, hear about what's happening in your region or town, and make connections in an appropriate and social setting.

7. Are you trying to branch out to a new industry sector? Follow the industry. Attend their business meetings and conferences, regionally and nationally, to meet prospective sponsors. Ask questions to learn what is important.

8. Take an active role on professional committees or boards that allow you to get to know new people, especially corporate leaders.

9. Volunteer in other settings, such as neighborhood or charitable events.

10. Be bold and contact someone mentioned in the local or regional media who seems appropriate for your opportunity. The more personal you can make this connection, however, the better and easier.

5 steps I'll take to secure new sponsors:

1.

2.

3.

4.

5.

5 Priorities for Improving Your Program

Improving your sponsorship program, especially if you suspect it lacks value, is an important and ultimately lucrative undertaking right now.

1. Assets

Many sponsorship programs only skim the surface of potential value they offer sponsors, and most do little to meet significant business or marketing objectives.

Let's face it. A logo in a sea of other logos on the back of a marathon t-shirt is not going to do a whole lot to improve a corporation's public image or to encourage sales. A package that includes a table for ten and name recognition in the event program book is really a charitable contribution with a set of tickets to the event. This kind of package is great for a company wishing to make a donation and has a rightful place in your resource development plans. However, it has nothing to do with *real* ROI, especially not in this economy.

Chances are the list of possible assets you *do* have to offer sponsors is more extensive than you realize. So, to get started, understand the value that you offer through the audiences with whom you have quality relationships. Then identify – or create – an inventory of assets that allows your partners to reach those audiences, interact with them, and develop a meaningful experience or connection.

Keep digging and probing. What else do you have to offer that is part of your core competencies, or is vital to your nonprofit mission, that businesses may find of value? For example, one client offers high-level sponsors access to a proprietary program that improves business leaders' acculturation when conducting business abroad, information that is inextricably tied to its own mission.

Another client, a New York-based hospital, had tremendous participation by its vendors in supporting its galas and golf events, but these underwriting opportunities did not represent the value of marketing-driven sponsorship. Furthermore, while the vendors courted the hospital's business, the hospital's development office lacked meaningful relationships with these donors and struggled to articulate the value of their sponsorship offerings.

As an interim step, before overhauling the entire program, we identified ways to enhance the program, including showcasing the donors' corporate citizenship in video messages, white papers, and through other publicity efforts that the hospital and sponsor's staff could easily implement. These pieces serve as testimonials by the hospital of the vendors as they seek new business outside the hospital.

Packaging Assets And
Meeting Your Sponsors' Needs

Get more creative with the ways you're packaging benefits. After researching and surveying your sponsors, you now have a better idea of the most pressing marketing and business needs your sponsors and prospective sponsors are facing. Ask yourself: "What challenges can our sponsorship program help overcome? What opportunities will our sponsorship program allow our partners to take advantage of right now?" Let the answers guide your thinking and the creation of your sponsorship package.

Then, as you package your assets and customize them for each sponsor, be sure you can evaluate your program using your client's metrics. How will you and they determine the ROI? Review the select list of 18 possible outcomes as a result of sponsorship on page 20. Which of your assets meet which outcomes?

Don't generate a generic sponsorship package that you

Asset Checklist

Review this list and see what new ideas for assets you may add to your program.

✔ **Communications materials:** brochures, flyers, posters, invitations, postcards, newsletters, informational packets, e-blasts, etc.
✔ **Public relations:** press releases and campaigns, press conferences, photo opportunities, press events.
✔ **Advertising opportunities:** print, radio, television, outdoor, web-based.
✔ **Onsite visibility:** banners, areas, booths, naming opportunities, sampling, concessions opportunities.
✔ **Event component opportunities:** naming rights, sampling, activities, hospitality, facilities, tours, venues, entertainment options, services, sales.
✔ **Promotional opportunities:** pre-event, post-event, official category designation, use of logo or trademarked name.
✔ **Deeper access with audience:** use of or access to database, hospitality opportunities, special offers.
✔ **Mission-related (for nonprofit organizations):** Areas of expertise, proprietary services or programs, enriched connection to philanthropic efforts.

mail or, worse, email out to the world. It's OK to have a sense of what your baseline packages will be, but develop individual plans for individual sponsors based on unique objectives.

Be sure that you are addressing the appropriate objective, especially if your sponsor is looking to streamline. If the sponsor needs a program with quantifiable results, such as building leads or generating traffic, don't provide a package that is nebulous or that offers only awareness-building benefits.

2. Marketing

Some organizations can benefit by improving the marketing and promotional efforts that support their events, festivals, conferences, and initiatives. All the ways you market your event and connect with – and expand – your audiences provide opportunities for your sponsors' benefit.

If you're promoting your event at the last minute, you lack a strategy. If you lack a strategy, you're missing opportunities to connect with ticket buyers, donors, registrants, or constituents, and you're not providing your event or your sponsors with full value.

If your marketing materials lack the visual or verbal message that tells your story, enhances your brand, and drives people to want to be part of your event or spon-

sorship opportunity, you've got two strikes against you. One, you're missing opportunities to connect and, two, you may be sending negative messages about what you have to offer, and therefore actually driving people away – including your sponsors.

Develop a long-term strategy and make a tactical plan that addresses who you want to reach, what you want to convey to them, and how you're going to do it. Commit this to paper a year in advance and apply resources to it. When you've determined what your marketing plans will be, you're almost there.

Next, you need to weave in assets from media partners, retail partners, and other promotional alliances you've created in the marketplace. Developing these types of alliances provide opportunities to build the buzz and extend your reach into your community. Plus they provide additional marketing cache to leverage with sponsors.

3. Know Your Audiences

Do you really know who comes to your event? Do you have a clear sense of who participates in the programs or activities of your organization? Can you describe these audiences in detail to your sponsors?

If not, now would be a good time to gain much greater

familiarity with your constituents or customers. Segment your audiences into groups based on relationships with your organization or event. Do you see patterns? Does your core constituency represent a particular demographic and/or psychographic profile? Can you break the group down into smaller sets? Do you have additional subsets?

Some sponsors are looking to reach mass audiences. When some food manufacturers launch a new product, for example, they cast a wide net and look for sampling opportunities at huge events (in the hundreds of thousands and larger). They would not be a likely target for an event that prides itself on having a niche market.

Events with niche audiences, however, are of keen interest to businesses looking for segmented exposure. A luxury car manufacturer may choose to sponsor an event whose audience is not large (perhaps 10,000 people) but that is affluent, educated, and a great match on many other segment-related measures. Conversely, the company may pass on free events with demographics that are too broad.

Examine your audiences, and you will learn where you have opportunities.

4. Fees Commensurate with Value

Pricing sponsorship is both art and science. Ultimately, it is based on the value your program provides to your partner, depending on the corporation's objectives and goals. The fee has nothing to do with how much something costs you, though certainly factoring in hard and "soft" costs, such as materials and labor, respectively, is important.

Consider the new realities of your sponsors' situations. They indeed may have experienced budget pressures and reductions. They may also need to see modifications to your sponsorship program to generate more solid results, or a new set of outcomes. They may need to expand one area, while contracting another. Or they may require streamlining altogether.

One of your responsibilities is to protect the value of your sponsorship program, no matter what, so that the program's value has integrity across the board for all your sponsors. If a sponsor requests a reduction of the fee, your question should not be, "should I cut the fee or not?" Rather, this calls for an exploration of what is to be accomplished. If, indeed, the sponsor is working with a lower investment level, look for ways to reduce the commensurate value as well.

If the sponsor is requesting higher value – moving from an awareness-building program to one with more measurable results, greater inclusion in more promotional opportunities, and greater opportunities for engagement with current or new customers – the fee should be increased, not reduced. A restructuring of the sponsor's entire program may be required.

What to research about your audiences

Where do they live?

Why do they attend your event?

What ethnicities do they represent?

What do they do for a living, and what is their marital or partnership status?

Are they older or younger?

Do they have children?

What is their household income?

What are their buying patterns for key purchases?

Do they live in the city or suburbs? Rent or own?

41

In addition, providing options or "add-on" features allows the sponsor to choose how much value it is prepared to invest in. And don't forget to suggest more flexible payment terms, for sponsors you trust, and to recommend payment in other forms, such as in-kind contributions.

5. Tone Things Down

Corporations may choose to operate in a more low-key manner, so as not to raise red flags with the media and with politicians, or others they fear who may make inflammatory comments. Discuss how to handle certain benefits, like hospitality and client entertainment.

It may be better for a sponsor to host a simple reception, rather than a more elaborate party. Or the sponsor may choose to host a breakfast or lunch meeting, with emphasis on an educational component. Outdoor events and festivals may provide a perfect picnic setting. To boost morale, your sponsors may want to extend the hospitality benefits to sponsors' employees.

Work with your sponsor or prospective sponsor to develop appropriate and effective plans. Certain industry sectors benefit tremendously from opportunities to interact in a relaxed environment and to build cordial and trusting relationships with clients and customers. Even in this politically fraught environment, sponsoring organizations and events is an effective way for a company to accomplish this goal.

Don't keep your program enhancements and new value a secret. Let your current or returning sponsors know about the new opportunities they might be interested in and about the new marketing endeavors that will improve the event and, ultimately, benefit them.

5 ways I'll improve our sponsorship program:

1.

2.

3.

4.

5.

Competent staff: Possesses marketing and sales/business development experience; able to sell service of an intangible nature. Project management and/or event management experience to execute and fulfill sponsor value.

Marketing Operation. How you market and attract customers, event-goers, or other constituents to your organization is central to the value you offer sponsors.

Sponsorship "Product." What is it that you have to exchange? How will you meet sponsors' goals and objectives?

Procedures and customer service guidelines. Your staff must understand how you conduct business, then act accordingly.

5 Opportunities to Enhance Your Operation

Developing a corporate sponsorship program for your event, festival, and/or other nonprofit program or initiative should be a strategic decision for your organization. You must have something of value to exchange with the corporate sector along with a competent operation to deliver it.

Is your operation all that it could be? Do you, or does your staff, make business development an art form? Do you have procedures and an infrastructure that supports all the ideas you generate for your sponsors? If a new sponsor called tomorrow, can your team identify the next 5 steps, after saying "hello"?

How your organization interacts with your corporate clients, through every step of the process, says a great deal to them about what to expect from the sponsorship experience with you. Using this time to solidify or enhance your operation will be to your benefit in the long run.

1. Knowledge and Competence

Everyone on your sponsorship team should be conversant about your organization's sponsorship opportunities and policies. They should be able to answer questions about who your audiences are, about the value of your opportunity, and about the different ways corporate partners may participate in your program. Someone in a supervisory role must be empowered to make decisions, especially during delicate negotiations, in order to protect sponsor value and optimize opportunities for your partner.

Sponsorship requires comfort with selling the intangible, along with a keen sense of ideation, or the ability to pair disparate concepts or ideas and create something new. Conceptual or abstract thinking skills are also essential.

2. Customer Service and Relationship Cultivation

What are the values that will imbue your sponsor relationships? How will you put this vision into practice?

Identify who on your staff is responsible for each relationship, during all phases of the sponsorship process. From the time the sponsor contacts you, or you contact them, be clear on your sales process, where you are along that process, and what signs indicate you're ready to move to the next step. Once you land the sponsor, who works with them? How will you organize your internal communications process so that the sponsor is channeling instructions and requests, and providing needed information, through one person, not many people?

How will you continue to work with your sponsor, both onsite at the event and through the evaluation period and beyond? How will you grow the relationship? How will your internal activities be focused, budgeted, and evaluated?

If there is a problem, how will it be handled? Who in upper management, if not you, will interact with the sponsor's upper management and build a relationship at the top? How will your board interact with sponsors? What is their role?

Sponsorship activation is still an important ingredient of sponsorship, despite the economy; however, like many businesses and operations, your partner may be facing staff shortages. What can you recommend to streamline the activation operation? Can you outsource the staffing, weaving the cost into your proposal? Can you provide volunteers to help out in some way?

Finally, how can you encourage your sponsors to work together, to extend the benefits and value of their participation with your event or organization even farther by working together? Organize your sponsors around a joint promotion. Share or leverage opportunities from another partner. Make introductions to develop a corporate community around your sponsorship opportunities and engage your partners.

Ideas like these show you're willing to go the extra mile for your sponsors. You and your team display a level of professionalism and respect for your partners that will be noticed.

3. Audience Research

Investing in research, even if gathered using low-cost or free online tools, can provide you with great information that will support your sales process and provide corporations with evidence they need to confirm a fit.

Minimally, gather demographic information about the people who participate in your sponsored events or programs. Find out what they like about your event or program, why it's important to them, and what else they'd like to see happen.

More in-depth research might include buying patterns, sponsor recall and perceptions, and greater insight into their future buying patterns, particularly in the midst of the recession and even as we move toward a rebound.

Develop a summary piece for your support materials, highlighting particularly relevant information for each company, whether a current or prospective sponsor. This will help your corporate partners understand your constituents and the importance of your mission, as further support of business goals of theirs.

For example, if your mission promotes environmental stewardship, do you have information or recommendations that might benefit your sponsors' operations? Sharing this information also furthers your mission.

Finally, as you collect data on the marketplace, on your sponsors' competitors, and on other issues that affect your operation or event and sponsorship program, use it to support your sponsor relationships. Share the information and engage in meaningful conversations with your sponsors.

4. Timing

Sponsorship requires a long lead-time to both secure and fulfill all the value – for your sponsors' and for your operations. You need to be working on sponsorship development at least six to nine months out for existing events and 12 to 18 months for new events. Here's why:

- Did you ever notice the length of time it actually takes to reach someone and schedule an appointment? You call them and reach voice mail. They call you and get your voice mail. And on it goes. By the time you finally sit down and talk, two months may have elapsed.

- The relationship and sponsorship cultivation plus negotiation processes come next. Factor in another two to six months.
- When you finally land the sponsor, you need to allow enough time to weave your new sponsor, depending on their level of commitment, into all your sponsorship opportunities. You may be advertising or marketing six months to a year out from your event.
- Likewise, your sponsor needs time to weave your sponsorship opportunity into its marketing and retail (or other) operations, too.
- If your sponsor contributes in-kind value as part of their fee, you need time to weave this value into your operation.

You get the picture. Don't even think about looking for a sponsor for an event that is less than six months away, unless you have an extraordinarily high-level of trust and an excellent relationship with the decision maker.

5. Your Event and Initiative Itself

Sometimes annual events become boring and stale because their producers, too, have become bored. They take their events for granted or simply lack the ingenuity to keep them fresh and interesting and attractive.

Be honest. How's your event looking? Is it still a dynamic

operation, bringing your community together? Is there a buzz in your community? Do people look forward to it? Does it sell out or do the hotel rooms nearby sell out? Are you attracting younger, fresh audiences?

If your event has become a little lackluster, now would be a good time to give it a good polishing. Take a walk through the event, in your imagination, and experience it wearing your customers' shoes. Now try on your sponsors' shoes. What can you do to improve it, make it more relevant, and make the event a desirable investment for your customers and corporate sponsors?

Get even more radical. Does your event need to be scrapped and replaced with something new? Would people miss it if it didn't happen? Could it merge with another event or conference to bring new life to it? See what ideas emerge from this investigation.

If your organization involves corporate partners into other initiatives, unrelated to events, evaluate them in similar ways. Are these activities fresh and relevant now? Do you and your sponsors feel energized through your collaborations? Are these initiatives critical to your mission and strategy? How else could you bring your partnership to life?

How about:
- a joint research study?
- a volunteer or community service project?
- a web-based conference or teleseminar, or series?
- jointly written white papers or special reports?
- membership drive with incentives from the sponsor?

What ideas create an opportunity that benefits your audiences, your sponsor, and your organization?

Now is the time for the hard decisions. And lots of creativity.

5 ways I'll improve our sponsorship operation:
jump-start

1. _____
_____
_____

2. _____
_____
_____

3. _____
_____
_____

4. _____
_____
_____

5. _____
_____
_____

Creating a Culture that Supports Sponsorship

Sponsorship is most effective when it is supported culturally. Otherwise, it is subject to internal sabotage and external rejection and yields poor results. Assuming you've decided strategically to build a valuable program for your corporate clients and to derive revenue from it, you must invest time and energy in creating an organizational culture that will support your program.

What if your internal or external culture has not been 100 percent supportive? Or what if it has been, but now you're seeing signs of anti-corporate sentiments? How can you change the landscape, internally and externally, to improve your program's success?

8 Steps to Improve Internal Culture

1. What are they saying? First, pay attention to conversations around the lunchroom and boardroom. What's being said? By whom? Ferret out negative comments, erroneous information, and other problems or potential obstacles.

2. What are the perceptions? Pay close attention to negative perceptions from staff, volunteers, and/or board members. What are the perceptions? What are they based on – deep-seated values or simply a lack of understanding, confusion, or misinterpretation of economic news?

3. Educate your staff and board about sponsorship. Help them understand the role the corporate sector has in your operation. Make sure that they know what sponsorship is, what the boundaries are between your two operations, and the positive opportunities for partnership or enhanced leverage. Help your team understand how sponsorship, beyond the dollars, benefits your community. Don't force this issue or trumpet your rationale disingenuously. Provide information and allow your staff and board to reach agreement.

4. Emphasize your policies. Help your staff and board understand the principles that guide your decisions about the kinds of companies with which your event or organization will partner. Better yet, involve the staff and board in making these decisions. Align with companies whose values and brands, not to mention demographics and goals, match yours.

Policies are easily made when a company's mission or values are completely different from yours. For example, if your core mission is promoting world peace, you're not going to engage in a partnership with a defense contractor. But, if you're an environmental organization, say the Sierra Club, will you accept sponsorship from a household products company, say Clorox, to promote their new environmentally friendly brand? (They did.)

You, your staff, and your board should reach a consensus. If there is dissension within your team, that same conflict may arise with external audiences, too. Then your sponsorship intentions and actions may backfire, leading to negative outcomes.

5. Establish customer service policies. As part of your overall strategy, define the type of relationships you want to have with your sponsors. What values will influence your relationships? What set of guiding principles will dictate your actions? Work with your staff to disseminate these policies and procedures throughout your event staff so that everyone understands the expectations.

6. Communicate with staff and board. Inform your staff and board about the current economic conditions and the factors that affect your sponsorship program. Let them know the actions your organization or event will take and what your expectations are for their participation. Invite them to contribute ideas and to be your organization's eyes and ears.

7. Engage your board as ambassadors. Your board members have a wide network in the public and private sectors, along with relationships with the media, your community, your customers, and your donors. Develop a set of activities and initiatives they can undertake in their day-to-day lives. How can they communicate a positive message about your sponsorship program that clarifies mistaken beliefs or opinions?

8. Update your sponsors. Let your sponsors know about these discussions and the steps you're taking to improve your internal culture. Work together to resolve critical issues, and act on any suggestions your sponsor has for you that are reasonable and workable.

8 Steps to Improve External Culture

1. What are they saying? Just as with your internal culture, you must keep your radar alert to hear what people in your wider world are saying. Listen for negative comments and anti-corporate sentiment; separate the uninformed rants from the comments that may have some important feedback under the surface.

2. Where and when do the comments appear? Are you seeing comments in blogs or in the comments sections of online newspapers? In Letters to the Editor sections? In online forums for your events? Calls to your office? Or more randomly, out in the world? The closer to home the negative comments are, the more readily you'll be able to respond. Have the comments occurred as a response to an isolated news event or to a bigger political drama? In either case, follow the stories and comments.

3. Educate the public and your constituents. Should your organization participate in this conversation? If so, how? Submitting your own letter to the editor, posting a blog entry, or issuing an online comment may be an excellent contribution to the public dialogue. However, check with your sponsor and its PR team first – assuming the commentary focuses on a company – to determine the best strategy together. Alternatively, you may conclude that working behind the scenes to overcome misunderstanding, conflict, or even guerilla marketing tactics against your organization or your sponsor could have a greater impact.

4. Use your communications tools, such as your newsletter, web site, blog, and certain events, to educate your audiences about corporate sponsorship. Mention your sponsors' role in your organization. Talk about how your sponsors contribute to your events' proceeds, which benefit your constituents and mission; and how this revenue ultimately benefits your community's enjoyment of your festival, program, or initiative. Be sure to mention the intangible benefits, such as the goodwill created by your corporate partners, how sponsorship programs allow you to expand your marketing reach, or expand programs and initiatives, because of the leverage the corporate sector brings to the table. Avoid being confrontational or argumentative, but don't be overly optimistic or patronizing.

5. Share your policies. Emphasize to your audiences the policies you have in place about accepting sponsorship dollars only from those companies that share your organization's values and commitment to your mission.

6. Take your message to wider audiences. To influence even wider audiences and educate them about sponsorship and to counter the recent political rhetoric, find other forums for your message. For example, offer a brief talk about corporate sponsorship for your Chamber of Commerce or other organization, whose members include business, governmental, and nonprofit leaders.

7. Be proactive. When you encounter public relations problems, bring them to your sponsors' attention. Advise them on the best ways to communicate with your audiences. Provide input and participate in the dialogue with your sponsors' team, including their public relations staff, to determine the best approach for handling a situation.

If appropriate, apprise your other sponsors of the situation through a simple top-line summary. This update will answer their questions, and you'll earn their respect and trust through your exemplary behavior. (Discussing the situation with your other sponsors should be a strategic decision and one that preserves confidentiality. In some circumstances, it may be preferable not to speak with other sponsors, to address the problem quietly and move on.)

8. Do your sponsors know? Be sure to share these external communications efforts with your new and existing sponsors. Make these kinds of activities a regular part of an ongoing public relations initiative.

5 ways I'll improve our internal & external culture:

1.
_____

_____

2.
_____

_____

3.
_____

_____

4.
_____

_____

5.
_____

_____

It All Starts with You

This is not the time to give up, assuming that the best days of corporate sponsorship are behind us.

Selling sponsorship when times are good is, of course, much easier. During difficult economic times, the process and principles are the same; however, your attitude, approach, resolve, and conviction must strengthen to match the challenge. You cannot control certain external conditions, but you can address conditions like deficient value or weaknesses in your operation that will hamstring your efforts if ignored.

You need a healthy dose of creativity to see possibilities where others don't. You need your imagination to work full-time right now, making connections where you previously hadn't noticed them.

You need to be persuasive. Build a business case. Address your partner's needs, one at a time, focusing almost exclusively on them, and then make the desired outcomes happen. Tweak constantly to get the results and returns they need.

You need to be relentless. Don't believe the argument that there's no money available. Demonstrate that your sponsorship opportunity has value and that it deserves the investment your sponsor can make.

When you land sponsorship deals, do what you say you're going to do. Hold your sponsors accountable and remind them of the importance of the ROI, of the measures they told you were important. If you reach obstacles and roadblocks on execution, go back to the basics: be creative, persuasive, and relentless.

You know how to do this. If you're an event or festival producer, you're already tremendously creative. You are able to think quickly on your feet and do whatever it takes to make something work.

If you're in development and nonprofit fundraising, you already know how to think like the other, a funder, a donor, or, in this case, a sponsor. You know how to find the hot buttons and push them. And then push some more.

If you're in marketing, you know how to invent and innovate, to survey the landscape, to see opportunities, address your customer's needs, and convey value persuasively.

If you're in the nonprofit sector, you know how to be resourceful, to accomplish big plans with limited means. You know how to galvanize support for your mission.

Will you muster the energy, strength and resolve to do what's necessary right now to protect your sponsor relationships and to preserve and grow your sponsor revenue? If you do, loyal partners who trust you, who invest in your events, festivals, conferences, and programs, today and in the future, will be among your rewards. I'd say the answer to that question is a no-brainer. Get busy. You've got some jump-starting to do!

Notes

1 "Financial Services Democrats Call on Northern Trust to Repay TARP Funds," press release in Newsroom section of House Committee on Financial Services web site, February 24, 2009. http://www.house.gov/apps/list/press/financialsvcs_dem/press0224095.shtml

2 "After Northern Trust 'Party,' Kerry Introduces Legislation to End Lavish Spending by Bailed Out Banks," press release in Newsroom section of Senator John Kerry's web site, February 24, 2009. http://kerry.senate.gov/cfm/record.cfm?id=308559

3 "Text of S. 463: TARP Taxpayer Protection and Corporate Responsibility Act of 2009," February 24, 2009. http://www.govtrack.us/congress/billtext.xpd?bill=s111-463

4 Sen. Kerry's February 24, 2009, press release.

5 "An Open Letter to Northern Trust Shareholders, Clients and Staff from Frederick H. Waddell, President and Chief Executive Officer of Northern Trust Corporation," About Northern Trust, February 24, 2009. http://northerntrust.com/pws/jsp/display2.jsp?XML=pages/nt/0902/1235518794634_466.xml

6 Ibid.

7 Anthony Malakian, "Sponsorship Scare Some Despite Revenue Upside," US Banker, March 1, 2009. http://www.americanbanker.com/usb_article.html?id=20090424YFRKLTZY

8 Allan Sloan, "Not Every Corporate Trip is a Boondoggle," Fortune, March 11, 2009. http://money.cnn.com/2009/03/11/news/economy/lavish_business_affairs.fortune/index.htm

9 Paul Gores, "Johnson Bank says no to T.A.R.P.," Journal Sentinel, March 5, 2009. http://www.jsonline.com/business/40793652.html

10 Ibid.

11 Eric Dash, "10 Large Banks Allowed to Exit U.S. Aid Program," The New York Times, June 9, 2009. http://www.nytimes.com/2009/06/10/business/economy/10tarp.html?_r=1&scp=1&sq=10%20banks%20tarp&st=cse

12 Sloan, "Not Every Corporate Trip is a Boondoggle."

13 Ben Stein, "Don't Blame the Business Trip," Everybody's Business, The New York Times, March 21, 2009. http://www.nytimes.com/2009/03/22/business/22every.html

14 Nick Clark, "Sponsors Slam on the Brakes," Business Analysis & Features, The Independent, February 10, 2009. http://www.independent.co.uk/news/business/analysis-and-features/sponsors-slam-on-the-brakes-1605498.html

15 Ritaf, Comments section of blog post by Mike Armstrong, "Got TARP money? Don't sponsor golf tournaments," February 24, 2009. http://www.philly.com/philly/blogs/phillyinc/Got_TARP_money_Dont_sponsor_golf_tournaments.html

16 Maria Aspan, "Sponsoring Arts Could Lose Luster," American Banker, March 19, 2009. http://www.americanbanker.com/printthis.html?id=20090318A72RTMZ3&usb=truei.constantcontact.com/ability.gov/

17 Performance Research, "As Consumers Tighten Their Belts, They Expect Corporate Sponsors To Do The Same," February 2009 Research Study. http://performanceresearch.com/companies-in-crisis.htm

18 Jeff Gelles, "Higher Hopes," Philadelphia Inquirer, p. C-1, May 27, 2009.

19 Lesa Ukman, IEG's Complete Guide to Sponsorship (Chicago: IEG, Inc., 1999), 1.

20 For a great example of this power, see my article, "The Power of Sponsorship," available at http://gailbower.com/pages/article_sponsorship.php.

21 Bob Diddlebock, "Why Businesses Are Still Giving To the Arts," Time, April 30, 2009. http://www.time.com/time/magazine/article/0,9171,1894971,00.html

22 "Cold Hard Facts: IEG/Performance Research Study Documents Economy's Effect on Sponsors," IEG Sponsorship Report, March 9, 2009.

23 James Surowiecki, "Hanging Tough," The New Yorker, April 20, 2009. http://www.newyorker.com/talk/financial/2009/04/20/090420ta_talk_surowiecki

24 "Summer Blues: IEG Revised Spending Forecast Cuts Growth Rate In Half." IEG Sponsorship Report, June 08, 2009.

25 Micheline Maynard, "Industry Fears U.S. May Quit New Car Habit," The New York Times, May 30, 2009. http://www.nytimes.com/2009/05/31/business/31car.html?_r=1&hp

26 See my article, "Too Small for Corporate Sponsorship? Think Again: How Your Business Benefits, Just like the Big Guys," in the Get BowerPower section of my web site, GailBower.com. It's an informative piece to share with your small and medium-sized business prospects to educate them on sponsorship.

About Gail Bower

Gail Bower is President of Bower & Co. Consulting LLC a firm that assists nonprofit organizations and events/festivals nationally and internationally in dramatically raising their visibility, revenue, and impact.

She's a professional consultant, writer, and speaker, with nearly 25 years of experience managing some of the country's most important events, festivals and sponsorships and implementing marketing programs for clients. These include Philadelphia's USAir Jambalaya Jam, RiverBlues, and Mellon Jazz Festival; New Orleans Jazz & Heritage Festival; Essence Music Festival; JVC Jazz Festival (Newport, New York, Miami); and the largest public events of former President Clinton's 1993 and 1997 Inaugurations, among others. Launched in 1987, today Bower & Co. improves the effectiveness and results of clients' marketing strategies, events, and corporate sponsorship programs.

She teaches event sponsorship seminars for Temple University's School of Tourism & Hospitality Management and speaks regularly about sponsorship, marketing, and events. Gail is a trusted source for the media, quoted in *Time* magazine, Meeting Professional International's *One+* magazine, *Direct Marketing News*, and online at *The Chronicle of Philanthropy*, and others.

To learn more:

- Visit GailBower.com.
- Subscribe to *BowerPower Papers*, a free quarterly e-newsletter, and access articles and special reports at the "Get BowerPower" section of GailBower.com.
- Participate in an extended dialogue on sponsorship and on *How to Jump-start Your Sponsorship Strategy in Tough Times* at Gail's blog.
- Subscribe to Gail's blog, SponsorshipStrategist.com.

To order *How To Jump-start Your Sponsorship Strategy In Tough Times*

To order additional copies of *How To Jump-start Your Sponsorship Strategy In Tough Times*, please visit **GailBower.com/jumpstart**. You may order safely and conveniently with a credit card through PayPal, and you'll also find a downloadable order form to use a personal or institutional check. The price of a single copy of *How To Jump-start Your Sponsorship Strategy In Tough Times* is $12 plus shipping. For orders of 25 or more, Bower & Co. offers a discounted price of $10 per copy plus shipping.

Please note, if you need to place a rush order, make special arrangements, make a gift purchase, or are interested in having Gail Bower speak at your organization's conference, upcoming meeting, or even to your board and senior leadership, **please call Gail directly at 215/922-6937.**